Tales Of México
Volume 1

DAVID ZELNAR

Designed By

DEDICATION

For my brothers. Since you were little, I have enjoyed reading you stories and I will continue to search for new ones to tell you.

CONTENTS

ACKNOWLEDGMENTS

First of all I would like to thank my parents, who have always supported me as I chased my dreams. I would like to thank my brother Zachary for joining me on my first trip abroad and joining me initially on the Mexican adventure. I would also like to thank my brother Levi for giving me the idea of moving to Mexico to search for stories to tell. A debt of gratitude goes out to the Mexican people for sharing their tales with me and embracing me as if I was one of their own. I have felt nothing but warmth and compassion from the people here and I hope my stories reflect this hospitality. Also, a special thanks goes out to all of my family and friends who have encouraged me along the way. And to Pumpkin, thank you for fixing my compass and adding to the perspective of my canvass by adding colors I never knew existed before, minus the blue of course.

INTRODUCTION

Hello, my name is David Zelnar, and I have spent a little more than a year in México searching for tales that caught my imagination. As a student of history, I wanted to find stories from throughout the past that still influence modern México. The stories you are about to read come from the Mexican people and are true to their history. You will witness some events beyond belief to the majority of skeptics but, at some point in society, were believed to be true by the people who told them. So keep an open mind while you discern if a story is fact or fantasy, and let's begin our first excursion through the magical world of México.

David Zelnar

We begin our journey at the jungle's edge in the Southern regions of México. No pyramids have been erected yet; nature rules this land. Human civilization will not appear for many years to come. We venture deeper into the wild to virgin territory where no man has ever stepped. We pass through a clearing and come across one of the most misunderstood creatures in the animal kingdom. Today it spends most of its time hiding in the deep recesses of caves, but this was not always so. The following tale tells the origins of this nocturnal hermit's descent into darkness. An animal among those in flight, but alone, with no other creature that was...

OF

A

FEATHER

In a land full of animals, before man's touch, there lived a Bat. This Bat would soar the sky from the desert in the north to the rainforest in the south, and it noticed that it wasn't like the other winged creatures. The others' skins were covered in plumes of every color, brightly shining in the sun: while the Bat's skin was bare and exposed, dull to the reflections of the light. The Bat decided that it wanted to look like the other birds, so it flew to the heavens to ask the Creator for feathers.

But, the Creator denied the Bat feathers of its own. The Guardian Above told the winged mammal that if it wanted plumage, then it would have to ask the Birds for theirs. The Bat took the task with delight; it planned to scour the land to find the most beautiful feathering anyone had ever seen.

First, the Bat approached the Flycatcher and asked for just one of its feathers. The Flycatcher agreed and gave the bat a small gift of yellow from its chest. The Magpie saw this and gave the Bat one of its blue feathers, as did the Yucatan Jay. The Bat received orange from the Oriole and the Bunting, the darkest shades of black from the Cacique and the Toucan, and purple from the Honeycreeper.

The Trogon gave him a green, a white, and a red feather. He was gifted the bright colors of the Euphonia, the Tanager, the Parrot, and the Macaw. The Quetzal and the Flamingo decorated the Bat in long feathers of pink and green.

The Owl gave the Bat's chest white-tipped browns, and the Woodpecker gave it a crown. The Hummingbirds sprinkled the Bat in green and cinnamon, and finally, the Motmot gave the bat's tail a stunning extension of a blue-green paddle.

The Bat was indeed the most magnificent creature in all of the land, and it was immensely proud of this fact. It made sure that every animal saw its spectacular colors as rainbows danced in the flutter of its wings. The beasts were entranced, for the Bat was covered in the most exquisite array of colors imaginable; it was mesmerizing. No creature's plumage, fur, or scales could rival the remarkable feathers of the Bat. The animals began to praise the glorious being. The Bat was now beautiful, and it achieved what it had always desired; to be admired.

But over time being consistently berated with compliments, the Bat began to feel superior to the other creatures, even those whose feathers it adorned. The arrogant Bat would strut in front of the Birds and contrast its beauty to theirs.

It would demean the birds for not being as impressive and tease them and tell them they were lesser. Ego had consumed the Bat, and its taunts became its only source of communication. The Bat's behavior was becoming intolerable.

One day the Creator called the beautiful Bat to the sky. The Bat was ecstatic; its gorgeous feathers had finally attracted the eye of the One Above.

The Creator must want to praise the beauty of the compilation of feathers that ornament my body, thought the Bat. It believed that it could dazzle the deity with its colors.

The Bat rose above the clouds to the heavens to show off its beauty. It flapped hard and with purpose as it climbed the sky. Higher and higher to the reaches of the Creator, the Bat pushed its wings with all its might. With each pull against the wind, a feather would fall. The determination of the Bat blinded it from its steady molting. It must show the Creator how beautiful it was, that was all that consumed its mind. But by the time it reached the heavens, there was not a feather attached to its body.

The Bat was just as it was before: dark, furry, with veined skin across its wings. Disgusting in its own eyes.

Below, the clouds became kaleidoscopes as a flurry of feathers danced through them. The snowfall of plumage lasted for two days.

Each colorful snowflake floated on its lane in the wind, gently settling after the whimsy of weather and aerodynamics.

The embarrassed Bat fled from the sky and returned to the surface, unable to collect its treasured wears. In fear of being spotted by the other animals, the Bat fled to the deepest caves and hid from its peers. The Bat went to the darkest part of the cave and refused to leave.

It gripped the ceiling with all of its might; nothing could remove the Bat from its place in the cavern.

As time passed, the Bat remained in hiding, only coming out at night when it was less noticeable. The Bat spent so much time in the darkness that it lost the ability to see color, forever blind to the beautiful creature it once was.

This tale is a reminder that we should never let our ego take control of us and continues to be told to children today. I personally had an issue with egocentricity when I first arrived in México and was called a "Yo, yo" due to my infatuation with telling stories about myself. But I digress.

We now fast forward in time to the height of the Aztecan alliance and its dominance over much of the land. Through my time here in México, I have heard many versions of a story about a woman wailing in the distance. Many tell of her being a distraught phantom crying for eternity after drowning her children. The reason for her committing such an atrocious act varies from tale to tale but usually deals with a man breaking her heart, and she murders their children in revenge or desperation. She is then forever doomed to roam the earth weeping for her lost children. There are even tales of her stealing the children of those who hear her or luring men to death.

I decided to look further into this woman's tale and found out that it goes much deeper into Mexican history than a simple ghost story.

The Nahuatl tell a story of her first appearing just before the Spanish arrived as a warning of the terror that will come. We arrive in Tenochtitlan in 1509, ten years before Cortez lands in Veracruz and begins his invasion of harrowing disease and genocide.

The Aztecan capital is booming with life and promise for the future, but this society needs to heed the warnings of…

LA
LLORONA

The vast empire spanned from the northern desert down to the edges of the jungle border with the Mayan states and chiefdoms; it reached from the ocean to the west across the continent to its endless coastline along the gulf. The city, protected by the surrounding mountains and volcanoes, controlled power over the land that made up this Aztecan alliance. Nahuatl was the lingua franca of the continuously expanding territory. From the palace on the lake, Moctezuma, the Second, sat upon the throne of the Tenochtitlan city-state as sovereign of the confederation.

The emperor took his daily walk to the twin temples and climbed the serpent staircase that led to the main altar for the afternoon ritual; there was not to be a sacrifice on this day. After his morning prayers, he made his way through the aviary past the hanging gardens to his bathing pool. Following his soak, he spent his day admiring his collections of plundered treasure, rare animals, and abnormal humans until it came time for his mid-afternoon feast. The aromas from hundreds of dishes filled the sprawling dining hall, Moctezuma consumed his favorites from his private dining area as he watched jugglers and acrobats perform. The lavishness was nothing but a typical day for the Aztecan ruler.

The Sun was beginning to set on Tenochtitlan; lanterns flickered to life throughout the city. Moctezuma watched the low glow from the homes reach towards the darkening sky from his overlooking balcony. The tranquility of the municipality brought a sense of comfort to the reigning Tlatoani.

"This is all because of me. The food in their bellies, the smiles on their faces, the safety they feel at night are all granted by my hand. It was divined by the Gods to make me the ruler of this land, but it is my own will that has made this empire the most spectacular the world has ever witnessed.

Nothing could destroy the harmony that lives in the union that I have built."

He basked in the reflection radiating from the glow of Tenochtitlan. Hearths were lit as the smell of meat and bread began to take control of the atmosphere, shades of orange bounced along the walls to limited shadows. Warmth radiated throughout the city as the families prepared to sit down for their evening meal.

Darkness hovered over the pulse pumping from homes into the streets. A flash of bright light pierced the darkest sector of the night sky. A fiery streak flew across the heavens residing over the city-state. The ball of fire lingered over the empire for all to see before descending beyond the horizon, dimming the city into confusion. The streets below filled as the glow from the comet consumed the night sky.

Moctezuma reveled in the confirmation of his divination. He believed that this comet was proof that the deities above approved, but his people had a different inclination about what this sign from above had inferred. Fear gripped the masses, murmurs grew to a roar; the Gods had been angered, and they were demanding resolution.

The citizens clamored to the palace, pleading for a sacrifice to appease the Gods for their transgressions. The fire in the sky must have been a warning to Tenochtitlan that if the proper sacrament were not made, there would surely be more to come. The crowd multiplied as more and more people joined the hysteria; a confused panic took hold of the Nahuatl population.

Now under the mercy of the tidal turn, the emperor was forced to comply and called his priests to order. He couldn't believe that the omen had led to such a panic.

A human sacrifice at the first sight of Huitzilopochtli approaching from the mountains was the only solution to appease the Sun God and, more importantly, the people.

"But my Lord, we are not to sacrifice a person for another dozen returns of the Sun. If we sacrifice too soon, we may upset the Gods even further." The head priest beseeched.

"Pay no mind to the schedule, the sky is on fire, and the people need reassurance that we are making the proper penitence to satisfy the Gods. At the first sight of Huitzilopochtli, a human sacrifice is needed to show the deities that we live in their homage. It will calm the masses and bring order back as it was this morning."

Just before dawn, the priests adorned in ritual plumage escorted a prisoner painted in smears of indigo to the upright stone slab atop the pyramid. The crowd at the base cheered as the man was stretched across the stone, exposing his bare chest to the sky. The head priest stood over the spread-out sacrificial man and began the ritual. The moment the Sun made an appearance, the priest drove his blade into the man's torso. As the blood poured from the body, the cleric jammed his hand into the incision and rose with a beating heart in his grasp. He presented the organ to the Sun as the lifeless body tumbled down the pyramid steps. The ritual sacrifice was complete, and the people believed that Tenochtitlan was safe from the wrath from above.

"You see. The Gods were not angry with us. They did not wish us harm. We have now gone for two days without another sign from them. My coronation was correct. I am Xiuhtecuhtli incarnate. The ball of fire was the deities reaffirming this to the people. The nation is not in danger from the spirits above." The Aztecan ruler declared.

His priests nodded and made their leave, afraid to contradict the Emporer. The head priest remained behind to consult Moctezuma on the coming days. The temperature suddenly dropped in the grand chamber.

"Looks like rain is coming," the priest informed his Tlatoani.

"Nonsense, this time of year?" Moctezuma rebutted.

No sooner had the words left his mouth than the sky opened up. The out of season storm consumed the city-state and began to growl at its inhabitants. Moctezuma stroked the turquoise idol of his patron deity and stared at the hearth pleading with the fire god in his mind. If there was one thing that would protect him, it was the spirit of the flame. Flashes illuminated the cloud-darkened sky until a loud crash reverberated through the city. A shock of electrical current exploded through the home of Xiuhtecuhtli, the same deity that Moctezuma had pleaded to for protection just moments before. Fear began to seep into his conscience. Perhaps the Gods were trying to tell him something.

The thumping rhythm of feet returned its march to the palace demanding explanation. With each moment, the thuds from heels meeting stone crawled deeper into the Tlatoani's core. He had tried to appease the wrong God and had omitted homage to his patron. The lightning strike upon his temple proved that Xiuhtecuhtli was disgusted with the tribute professed to him. If Montezuma did not appease this transgression, he knew that the wrath of the Gods would be met by the uprise of the people. He demanded another sacrifice in the name of the Lord of the Hearth.

The pyramid was adorned in turquoise as the propitiatory captive was positioned below the priest garnished in the same reverent stone. The ritualist plunged his blade into the man's chest, drawing his heart from the wound. Assistants quickly stuffed the cavity with kindling, and the priest returned with a torch. He lit the newly formed hearth of bone and flesh with the tip of the flame. The fire burned bright in the evening sky as the priest lowered the man's heart back to its original cavity. The pulsating muscle began to steam in the priest's hand; he reached above his head for Xiuhtecuhtli and all of Tenochtitlan to see it ignite.

The wrong had been corrected, and Xiuhtecuhtli had received proper veneration.

Moctezuma was now able to continue his daily routine as he had before. Just after breakfast, he climbed the serpent staircase to the twin temples of Huitzilopochtli to the South and Tlaloc to the North to perform his morning ritual. As the emperor neared the summit, he noticed a blurred mist surrounding the southern red temple. The cloud of heat thickened to an unbearable repellant before bursting into flames consuming the single twin temple. Moctezuma quickly realized that the Gods were not finished with him yet.

The Aztecan ruler was at a loss; the sacrifices did not satisfy the Gods. What were they trying to tell him? What did they want? He spent countless nights discussing the meaning of these occurrences with the clergy and questioning his divination in private. There had to be a reason for the Gods exposing their wrath, whilst sparing the lives of the Mexica people. Not one of his advisors could agree on a cause, let alone a solution. Moctezuma believed he would have to be the one to decipher the will of the Gods.

Soon after, he was to be tested by another out of season rain. It began with a drizzle that grew to a steady two-week pour. The island city began to sink below the waters of the lake. Streets became shallow rivers seeping into anxious homes.

Tlaloc was now showing his disdain for the Aztecan capital, while the emperor tried in vain to understand the signs before him. The rain eventually stopped, but Tenochtitlan had to wait for the flood to return to the lake, and the water was in no hurry to leave.

The nights were thick with the resonant stench from the slowly receding water. The mist held echoes in its droplets, wind, and whispers swam without escape. Rumors began to spread of a woman crying amongst the fog. More and more citizens began to reaffirm the chatter with accounts of their own experiences with the voice.

Theories that it was a cihuateteo giving warning caught the attention of the Tlatoani. He made a declaration to the people and instructed his calpixques, who had never faltered in carrying out his orders in the past, "To all of those in the habit of walking at night, if you come across a woman weeping do ask her why she cries so. What is it that brings her sorrow, and how can we ease her soul? A cihuateteo has much to be sullen for, after being taken by the battle of labor, but never has one become so recurrent.

She wants to tell us something; it is your duty to listen to her words."

It was but the next night when a young calpixque came with the news that he had encountered the cihuateteo continuing the flood with her tears as she stood at the crossroads of a street and a canal.

"And what did she say?

What does she want?" Moctezuma demanded.

"She simply stood there, sobbing, 'We are all going to lose. Oh my children, where can I take you and hide?' I don't understand my Tlatoani, hide from what? What could ever bring our great empire harm?"

"Do not worry, young man, as the reincarnation of Xiuhtecuhtli; I will not hide from any foe near or far. The Gods have given us warning, and we must be prepared for the great battle ahead."

Years passed without another sign from the deities. After nearly a decade, the omens had become hardly parlor talk about a time before.

Moctezuma had relaxed in the peace and had but all forgotten la Llorona's warning. He began his day per usual and climbed the serpent staircase to the peak of the pyramid with two rejuvenated temples.

The Aztecan ruler could see the mountains that protected his kingdom rising in all directions from the steps leading to the entrance of Huitzilopochtli's alter. A glimmer came glinting from the edge of the nearest slope. The Tlatoani squinted as he tried to get a more unobstructed view of the cause of the reflection in the distance. Standing tall on a bluff was a man with two heads and four legs staring back at him.

The odd creature came from another world armed for battle. His eyes fixated on Tenochtitlan like a Xoloitzcuintli waiting to be fed. Montezuma watched as the monster descended the cliff towards his home, another sign from the Gods he was sure.

The meeting of Moctezuma and Cortez was the first step of many that led to the end of local rule, as the Spanish displaced, murdered, and enslaved the people who originally inhabited the land. As the Spanish empire expanded, men were sent to every corner of the empire to guard their newly plundered assets forever reshaping the societies across the globe and, in this case, México.

Many of the religions before the indoctrination of Catholicism here believed in the supernatural and certain areas even having powers beyond explanation. Many thought they were gifts from the gods or even aliens. One such force that they believed was that some places possessed the ability to transfer goods and possibly people through some cosmic portal.

We are staying in Tenochtitlan, which is now referred to as Ciudad de México in Nueva España. It is October 23rd, 1593, and we are about to meet a man and learn about his miraculous journey to the conquered capital. This is...

THE
TELEPORTATION
OF
GIL PEREZ

Gil Perez was a man of duty. His life consisted of routine and schedule; he was a palace guard after all. Not being the most sociable of the colonizers, the simplicity of his day suited him just fine. He would wake in the early afternoon, consume some leftovers from the pot, and wander the grounds until it came time for him to man his post. Being a night guard, he was able to limit his human interaction, even though he enjoyed the short moments when he and his fellow guards' assigned routes crossed paths. He was content with his life in Manila: other than the rainy season, he despised the rainy season. He was glad he took up the guard and journeyed to this far away place.

The day was October 23rd, 1593, when the news came. The Chinese forced-oarsmen orchestrated a mutiny aboard Gómez Pérez's ship. A three-day plot led to the violent seizing of the galley.

Not realizing what caused the commotion, and merely believing it only to be more men manning the oars to steady the ship through rougher seas, the Governor stepped out of his cabin, his scalp bare to the wind, to three armed recently freed men who greeted him with every direction of their blades.

The colony was on the verge of tumult, and every guard was set to double shifts. A soldier or guard covered every thirty meters in a pacing motion only to break in assigned increments of every third bell's toll. The tenseness of the air alone could slow an uprising as the council rushed to elect a new leader. No one moved around the palace unless someone in uniform accompanied them. Stressed exhaustion took hold of the city.

Gil was heading for his second day of double duty since the assassination of Dasmariñas the night before. A simple widening of his eyes is all he could manage to acknowledge the other guards as he marched past them on his way to his post. Everyone reciprocated in a similar manner of his or her own. Diligence and uneasiness was the key to fighting a coup and the atmosphere filled with the suspense of waiting on what was to come. To Gil, this apprehension was beginning to hum.

He approached his assigned area for the evening, the outer corridor of the deliberation chambers. An arched walkway connected the garden and the executive, sixty steps long and twelve steps wide, a grand door blocking one end tunneling out to a sprawling maze of flora lit only by its lookouts.

This was Gil's area to protect. He was to march up and down, checking every opening for anything suspicious and out of place, although the chances of someone getting through one of these bush filled niches that lined the left wall undetected was unlikely. He began his march still tired from being on guard from the evening before to well into that morning. The hall was still, the wind stagnant. The strain of being trusted to protect this corridor pressed on Gil. With each glance through the floor to shoulder level spade window, Gil felt the constant anticipation of a Chinese dissident emerging from the shadows to further disrupt the colonial hierarchy. It was his job to stop him. The hum in his ears started to vibrate more violently; the sound grew intolerable. The room began to bounce in different directions leaving Gil queasy from the imbalance. He leaned against the wall to catch himself from falling into disequilibrium. He closed his eyes to center himself and drifted for a moment.

Gil's eyes flickered open, and the world around him pulled itself into focus, only the walls were missing. He took a couple of glances back and forth and furrowed his brow. How did he end up in the garden? He took a step forward, and the cool breeze caught him off guard, there was a lack of salt in the air. Gil shook his head. He must've been assigned this spot; the lack of sleep was just getting to him. But something was not quite right. The stone at his feet seemed to be a different shade, but that could be from the dizziness. But where were the walls? He swore he was leaning against a wall. Nothing was matching what he had just seen a few minutes prior. He tried to make sense of being in a different location, but his head was still spinning. He must have always been here, and he had just remembered the area wrong.

His head was playing tricks on him; this is where he was assigned. He measured out his zone; whenever he was stationed in the garden, four quadrants were always split on a cross, centered by a fountain. But where was the fountain, where were the plants or hedges for that matter? The garden was empty. The flat tile pattern continued unimpeded across the dimly lit courtyard until it was by lanterns hanging outside of buildings blurred in the distance. Gil stretched the grogginess from his body.

I must have been assigned this plaza, and the lack of sleep is why it looks unfamiliar, he thought to himself. He gripped his weapon and began his march around the center of the square. Coming from the building in the corner to his right, two guards came running towards Gil. Good, he thought, maybe my shift is over, and I can go home and get some rest. Gil started walking in the direction of the two men and could see tinges of red coming from their uniform. He grasped his weapon tighter, for his uniform was blue. The soldiers arrived with weapons drawn. Now being closer to the light, Gil could tell that even though their uniform differed, they were indeed Spanish.

"Who are you? And what are you doing here?" the man on the left shouted in a thick Castilian accent.

"I am Gilberto Perez of Aragon, sentry guard of this Governor's palace here in Manila."

"Señor, did you say Manila?

"Yes, and I demand to know why you are armed in differing uniform in the palace the day after our Governor was assassinated," Gil responded proudly of his composed behavior to these outsiders.

"But Señor, you are not in Manila," the second man said in an uneasy tone. Gil looked at this confused man with concern. "Señor, this is México."

México! What is wrong with this man? We are deep in the far eastern islands, and he thinks this is a land of pyramids. How could these men be so lost?

Two more guards noticed the standoff in the Plaza Square and approached the group with their weapons at half-wield. Gil noticed that he was quickly becoming outnumbered by these Spanish men uniformed in red. Is this an invasion? But why would the Spanish invade the Spanish?

"What unit are you from soldier? What brings you to México?" demanded the higher-ranked of the newly approaching guards.

Could it be true? Is it possible that I'm in México? But how did I get here? Why don't I remember? Confused Gil could only sputter out one question.

"What day is it?"

"Why it's the twenty-fourth of October."

"And of what year?" Gil mused at the idea that it was still the same day, yet he could be on the opposite side of the planet.

"The year of our Lord fifteen and ninety-three, of course."

"That's not possible.

I'm a palace guard in Manila, and I was just in Manila today. The Governor was assassinated yesterday. There is no way I can be in México. It's just not possible."

Gil was frantic. He was starting to believe that maybe he was in México. He dropped his weapon. Maybe it was magic. Maybe it was aliens. Maybe it was God. Maybe I'm mad. I woke up in Manila, I spent my day in Manila, now I'm in México. I was in Manila; now I'm in México. Do I have powers? Have I been on a ship this whole time? No, because the Governor was killed yesterday. Someone must be mistaken; you can't just appear in another place. But all of these men claim that this is not Manila, and I don't recognize anything, but it is dark. Gil could not place where he was with certainty.

The guards edged closer to the hysterical man self-debating into his palms. They slowly encircled the delirious misdressed guard and restrained him from three sides to allow the commanding officer to ascertain judgment on this distressed soul.

"Now calm down you. What is this of the assassination of your Governor? Speak up. Is what you say true?" the Captain demanded of his captive.

"Just yesterday, Gómez Pérez Dasmariñas, Governor of Manila, was killed in a mutiny aboard his ship. We believe it to be Chinese oarsmen who carried out the plan." Gil spouted out before he realized how insane he must sound. If it happened yesterday, then how did he get here today?

The Captain raised his brow at this odd response from the disturbed stranger. "Throw him into a cell for now. He seems to know something, but he is of no mind to make sense at present."

Gil was abruptly dragged to the street where a carriage was set with two more guards in red standing at its door; another manned the horse. A guard entered, and Gil was shoved into the seat next to him as the other guard sat to his free side. The two guards who initially found him sat on the bench across from the three of them.

The carriage took off as soon as the door slammed. Racing through the empty evening streets, Gil could see flashes through the window's curtain. This was definitely not Manila.

Gil's head jerked as his eyes opened. He was now sitting in the center of a damp cell with a window the size of his fist as the only source of sunlight. At least this gave him a sense of time; he just wasn't sure where this cell was located. Maybe he just dreamt all of that México nonsense, and now he's been imprisoned for abandoning his duties. But Gil would never abandon his post. He was there, and then he wasn't. Now he was in a cell and was not sure why.

Days passed, and the guards only came by the cell to drop off scraps of food, never answering Gil's pleas and questions. On the third day, the Captain entered with a guard and pulled a stool up next to where Gil was lying. He stroked his beard as he sized up his prisoner.

"So, are you going to tell us how and why you are in México?"

"I've told you. I was standing guard at the Governor's Palace in Manila, and I closed my eyes for a few seconds, and the next thing I know, I'm standing in the middle of your city's plaza. I don't know how. I really don't."

The Captain's temple curled as he raised his head, "Is this the same palace for the Governor you claim was assassinated?"

"Yes, and I know what you're thinking. But I'm a guard, and I would never do that. It is my job to protect the governor. He was on his ship when it happened, and they already got the ones who did it."

"And yet you arrive here with this news before any emissary ship from the Philippines. Why is that? It is quite suspicious, you know, announcing yourself in the center of the city nonetheless."

Gil scrambled to find a reasonable explanation but had no logical solution to present the Captain other than he just didn't know, and this was not satisfactory. The Captain stood up and shook his head. "Well then. We shall have to wait to see if an envoy from the East arrives to corroborate your story.

If not, you shall either be tried as a deserter or a witch, either of which must be true." With that, he exited not to be seen again by Gil for weeks to come.

As the weeks passed, the isolation gave Gil no other choice but to dig deeper into the question of how he got there. Every time he closed his eyes, he expected to be returned to Manila, but each retraction of the eyelid only sucked power from this hope. He must be a messenger from God, but what was his message? That the Governor was dead? It doesn't seem likely that God would waste his time with such a menial note. It's not like God works as a herald of the King, delivering newsagents around the world to keep the empire informed. No, it had to be something else.

Gil had no idea how long they would wait before deciding that he was a liar and shall stand trial as one. In the colonies, Gil would undoubtedly be viewed as a threat and would face execution or banishment to the elements. There the natives or Mother Nature herself would take his life in these newly charted territories. The freeze in the air suggested that he was not anywhere near the sea. It could take quite some time for a ship to arrive, and the news to reach the city of México. Each day hung the balance of wait, news, or death, wait always being the judgment.

The day finally came when the Captain ultimately entered the dungeon to give his verdict on the life of Gil Perez. He smiled as he approached Gil's cell. In a chuckle, he said, "I have news for you, Señor Perez. Do you believe in Christmas miracles, because an envoy from Manila has indeed arrived? And they came to deliver the news of the mutiny against Governor Dasmariñas. And a member of their crew even recognized your name."

The Captain waved at the door, and in came a guard dressed in blue. "Is this the Gil Perez you know from back in Manila?"

The man approached the bars of Gil's cage. Gil couldn't believe it; it was his neighbor for the past three years. He had to recognize him. The man looked and studied him as if he were inspecting a crime scene. Gil began to speak, but the man cut him off, "Well, of course, that is Gil Perez of the Manila Guard, but how did he end up here? Were you on the ship?"

The Captain interjected, "Quite the quandary. Old Gil here has been with us since before the local Day of the Dead celebrations, and we are now nearing Christmas. That must be two months now. Ah, yes, we found him on the twenty-fourth of October."

"But that can't be. I saw him on the twenty-third."

"Witch!" screamed one of the guards.

"Calm down, calm down," ordered the Captain. Then he quickly whispered under his breath, "Ok, I believe you."

Gil was still stunned, so he nodded, only partly understanding the meaning. The Captain pointed at the cell lock, "Open the gate and have Señor Perez escorted to his commanding officer at the port so he may return to his post."

Gil was surprised, but the other guards looked weary.

"Do it now!" The Captain exclaimed.

The two guards in red rushed to the order. Each took an arm under Gil's and directed him out of the corridor. The guard in blue followed shortly behind. They made their way to the stables for transport to the coast. An elderly stable hand offered little assistance.

"There is little I can do, I'm sorry. But I don't have a driver."

"Not an issue. We can manage the journey ourselves in a carriage," the eager guard proclaimed.

"But you're not listening to me, son. We only have horses ready to go. I have two bent axles and a loosened chassis."

"Fine, we will take four horses geared to reach the coast."

The group mounted and followed the sun to the horizon. Gil rode up front with his fellow man in blue while the two guards in red followed behind to keep an eye on the mysteriously appearing man.

"Psst, Gil. I have to know. How did you get here?"

"Seriously, I can't explain. It must have been magic."

There is no telling the disorientation these men must have felt being moved around the world. Think of the military now with a much higher death rate and much longer tours.

How Gil Perez arrived in México City in the early colonial period is still an unsolved mystery. Maybe the local people knew something about teleportation, and we simply never paid attention, or perhaps Gil simply suffered from memory loss due to PTSD from his long tours to hostile places that differ so significantly from Spain. I prefer to believe in alien magic.

A century has passed under the rule of the Spanish. We move northwest along the mountains to the city of Guanajuato during the colonial era in the 1700s, where being Spanish born and having 'pure' Spanish descent held clout. Loyalty to the crown was not in question. Your name landed you in a class, and you only associated with your kind.

The couple that we are about to meet is commonly known as the Mexican Romeo and Juliet. Their tale of a forbidden romance between the classes shows a dark side of Mexico that has remnants today. But despite the class divide between them, these two remained fervent in their belief in love.

We follow the cobblestone road, up the hill to the archway above...

THE
ALLEY
OF THE
KISS

"Do you see her, Miguel? Do you see that angel sitting in the church of God?" Luis prodded his annoyed friend praying next to him in the pew. "Oh what a creature, sculpted by God's hand itself. There is not a more mesmerizing sight in all of México. Nothing compares to the beauty that is Carmen." Miguel rolled his eyes. "Did you know Miguel that she rescues the strays from her Colonia? Ah, there is nothing in her soul that lacks perfection."

40

His friend scoffed, "So why don't you just go up over there and talk to her so you can stop this endless pining? We would all be better off."

"You of all people should know that that is impossible. Her father is one of the wealthiest landowners in the region. He demands that his daughter marries a nobleman from España, not a poor miner like me." Luis replied in despair.

"But Luis, my friend, you will never know if you never take a chance. Besides, what her father doesn't know won't kill him."

"Yes, but if he found out that I even talked to her, it might kill me."

"You're not as bad off as you're making it seem. You own your own home, don't you? "

"A shack of but two rooms on a tiny plot at the edge of town, not exactly a palace."

"But a home nonetheless. And you have steady employment at the mine, and with her father's connections, you could be running the place in a few years. If his daughter felt a smidgeon of what you profess to feel for her, then her father

41

would have to consent to the courtship. So go and at least let your presence be known."

Doña Carmen was standing near the altar with the housekeeper, her father's back turned to exclude them from the conversation of men. Her eyes wandered the room until they met Luis' staring from a pew many rows back.

She turned to the housekeeper; "There he is Nana, that rugged boy with the soft eyes who is always watching me. Oh, how I wish he would come speak to me. Perhaps I would find out why he looks at me so, it truly does make my heart race. But it will never take place; for Father would not permit me to converse with a man he has not arranged himself. What to do, dear Nana? His face haunts my dreams, I must know who he is."

The housekeeper sighed as she contemplated, always to her Doña's assistance, she would find a way to bring her this little joy.

"Ok so when he makes his way to exit, we will make sure we cross paths at the dish of holy water. You will have time to ask your question, but then we must leave before your father notices our whereabouts."

"Oh thank you, Nana." Carmen hugged the housekeeper. "What would my life be without you? My sweet, sweet Nana."

Miguel nudged his friend, "Hey, we better leave before that girl's father sees you gawking at his daughter."

Luis agreed and slid out of the pew to follow the procession of fellow believers away from the cross above the altar, each dipping their hands in the holy protectorate before making their leave. Luis had barely touched the water when he saw the reflection of an angel looking back at him. He lifted his head to see if he had imagined this vision. Standing across the pool, the creature that stressed the palpitations is his heart smiled, but he could barely squeeze out a hello.

"Who are you strange boy whose eyes are persistently affixed to my position?" Carmen whispered as she held back her giggles.

Luis' hand fell deeper into the water, "I am Don Luis, Señorita. I am sorry, but I can't help but stare. Your beauty distracts my faith in God."

The housekeeper placed her hand on Carmen's

back as an escort from the church. Carmen glanced over her shoulder as they joined the crowd of parting parishioners, "Don't be sorry, Don Luis." Then she was gone, and Luis was left with his hand in the holy water and his mouth agape.

Miguel came to the church's new statue attached to the bowl of holy water. "Luis, I think you've had your share. It's not a bath, you know."

Luis shook himself back to reality. "She was here, Miguel. She put her hands in the water at the same time that I did. She spoke to me. We talked. I think she feels the same way I do. But there is no way to tell. I have to speak to her again. Oh, her angelic voice. She is the one. God put us here together on purpose. Can you believe it; we finally spoke to each other. I am certain that we will be known as the world's greatest love story."

"What did she say?"

"Well… she just asked who I was and why I stare all the time. But I'm telling you, she feels the same way." Miguel just laughed at his love-struck friend.

Every Sunday, Carmen and Luis followed the same ritual, getting to know the other with well-placed words within a minimal allowance of time. Each response inched their hands closer to the center of the bowl. Electric as the water may have been, fear was still the barrier that kept the tips of their fingers from making contact. But even that barricade couldn't fight the current between them, and if only for a second, they eventually touched. The drums in their chest caused waves to lap the edges of the dish. Although limited, this time became the obsession they longed for throughout the week.

Eventually, their palms met beneath the surface. Luis took his other hand and washed Carmen's hand in the sacred liquid. Each drop caressed her skin as he gently stroked her knuckles with his thumb. They smiled at each other; a moment of bliss passed, and the world fell away.

Suddenly their embrace was severed, and she slipped from his tender grasp. "What is this? How dare you touch my daughter?" The abrasive landowner loomed above the two, Carmen's wrist clutched above her head as her father snatched her away from her beloved. "I give you anything your heart desires, and this is how you repay me, with the courtship of a commoner. You are not to leave the house until a proper suitor comes to call for your hand in marriage. You are not to see this filthy boy again. Am I understood? "

"But father, I love him. Please don't do this." Carmen pleaded with her father but to no avail. His reputation and status were his priorities, not the love fancy of his adolescent daughter. He dragged the young woman home and locked her inside her room. Her only contact would be with the housekeeper, and the closest she would get to being outside would be on her small balcony overlooking the alley. Here was where she was to spend her days until she moved to the home of a husband her father had chosen as worthy.

Luis returned to church every Sunday, and each week her father would arrive but without Carmen by his side. He had to see her, and if she couldn't come to him, he would go to her. Luis snuck his way out of the cathedral and ran up the cobblestone hill to her home. He hid in the shadows under the balcony and called up to his imprisoned love. But on Sundays, when she was refused the chance to see the boy who had possession of her heart, Carmen would fall ill to depression, and the only aid to her condition was being entombed in her blankets with high regiments of sob filled sleep. Luis' shouts were suffocated and never heard.

Luis would not be deterred by her lack of response. She was in there, and he was sure that she felt the same way. He just needed to find a way to get to her. He looked for scaffolding to scale or ropes he could climb, but the building afforded no access to her balcony. He eyed every inch of the building, looking for an access point. Only the window that hung across the alley, which was but arms reach from the balcony, gave any access to his dearest Carmen.

To his joy, he saw a sign in the window advertising that the apartment was for sale. He ran to the door below and began banging. A middle-aged man pushed back the door in anger. "What do you want? Making all this commotion. What is it that you need?"

"The room Señor, the one by the balcony, is it still for sale?" The man saw the desperation in Luis' face but refused to sell to him. "Go away, there is nothing here for you."

Luis was not going to be turned away so easily. He pressed the man, he persisted and pleaded until the irritated man finally gave in and gave Luis a price. But the price was highly inflated. The man figured hearing such a sum would get rid of this nuisance of a boy, and he could continue on with his day. But even though it was not feasible, Luis agreed to the man's ransom. He was forced to sell his home and everything he had of value to afford the room by the balcony. But he did so without hesitation, for he would soon be able to see Carmen, and that was all that mattered.

Carmen couldn't take her confinement any longer. Her resentment grew into hatred for her father. If she were not able to pick her own groom, she would defy her father and age into an unwed spinster. Her prison was beginning to enclose around her, her sobs were losing oxygen to continue. She needed room to breathe. She opened the doors to her balcony to catch her breath, and there stood Luis waiting at his open window.

She ran to the edge and clasped hands with her

love. The two were finally able to be together even if only at arm's length. They continued to meet nightly to profess their love while trying to figure out how they could be together forever. Each night they pushed the limits of the distance between the balcony and the window until they were able to stretch themselves to the point where their lips could finally embrace. The world around and below melted away, and the kiss was all that shined in the moonlight.

Carmen's absence from anywhere but her chambers irritated her father. The furious man had become fed up with his daughter's insolence, and possessive driven rage consumed the patron. She was to marry a man of wealth and with this union save his failing estate. He stormed up the stairs to her room, chest puffed in anger, only to be intercepted by the housekeeper waiting at the door.

"Out of my way, I need to talk to my daughter!"

"Oh, but sir, she is not feeling well. Do come back in the morning." The au pair pleaded.

"Nonsense! Move! My daughter will understand

if I have to beat it into her." He pushed the woman out of his way and forced the locked door ajar.

To his disgust, he saw his daughter leaning over the balcony kissing the very boy he had forbidden her from even speaking to. He stomped as he screamed in their direction, but the couple was still lost in another moment; his shouts fell before them like scattered snowflakes never making an impact. The sourly betrayed father pulled a dagger from the sheath hanging on his belt. In a lunge, he plunged the blade into his contemptuous daughter's back.

The two remained locked in their kiss, but Luis had noticed that Carmen's hand had fallen limp and cold. He pulled away to see her eyes fade as her blood-soaked her garment. She was slipping; he pulled her hand to his face. His lips were granted one parting graze before she fell away.

Her father stood above her lifeless body and glared at Luis. "This is all your fault that this has happened. You will suffer the same fate as her, no matter how far you run or how hard you hide. You will pay for the death of my Carmen."

Luis ran, and he ran to the only place he knew well; the mines. His brain could not cope with Carmen's murder at the hands of her father no less. He had done everything possible to be with her, and she was still taken from him in the end. He walked to the edge of the main shaft. They were supposed to be happy. They had found each other and fallen in love. This is not how it was their story was supposed to end. He stepped closer. They were meant to be together forever. He took one final step.

I warned you it was a tragedy. Classism still remains a major social issue in México, and this is a tale told to remind people that love should be able to conquer any barrier set before them by society. Unfortunately for Luis and Carmen, this hatred of the so-called "lesser" ended the way it did, and I'm sure they are not the only ones to befall this fate.

We move west to the city at the base of the mountains, Guadalajara. I have spent most of my time in México in this city, and while living there, I discovered a cemetery full of frightful tales of the supernatural that, as I entered its iron gates, chills crawled down my spine.

The revolution has already taken place, and México has been independent from Spain for some time now. The new country has moved into an era of prosperity in the late 1800s, and here we stand at the gates of the Panteón de Belén. We enter and pass the numerous graves to the far corner of the walled cemetery to ...

THE VAMPIRE TREE

"What is that?" Caesar asked his friend as he pointed to a hunched-over object in the road.

"I don't know. I think it's a dog." Alexis replied as the two inched their way over to the out of place creature. Unkempt fur curled around its tail, its body thin like it only housed a skeleton, almost as if it had been drained of all of its fluids without being cut. "Why do you think it looks like that?"

"I have no idea, but I bet I know who could help us. Inspector Espinoza. He would know exactly what happened to this animal." Caesar replied.

Alexis removed his poncho and wrapped the scrawny dog's corpse. The two boys scampered to the home of the inspector, 848 Calle Prisciliano Sanchez. The inspector's window abundant office/apartment capped the light green three-story building with a market at its base.

"Inspector, inspector, we have something to show you!"

The two boys put their hands to their brow to block the sun as they watched for movement on the inspector's rooftop patio. No one seemed to be there other than the dogs. The boys waited, sure that he must be home. A window, to the corner of the building, flung open, "Well what are you waiting for? If you have something, then bring it on up." The ends of the longhaired inspector whipped the pane before the startled boys could catch their breath. They quickly composed themselves, scooped up the poncho-draped pooch, and quickstepped up the stairs to the plated door of Inspector Espinoza. Alexis reached to knock, "Come in I don't have all day!" Caesar nervously reached for the knob and pushed the door into the inspector's office/living room.

Inspector Espinoza was standing at his desk on the far side of the room, glancing at assorted papers. "So what do you boys have for me?" he asked with arrogant intrigue. "It's something worthwhile, I hope."

"Si Señor," Alexis held up the wad of cloth as he walked across the room, "you're going to want to see this."

The inspector cleared an area from his desk, and the boy set his poncho on the empty space. Espinoza quickly unwrapped the putrid package to find the dehydrated canine cadaver in a mummified state of terror. But he did not seem to be impugned by the sight of the dog. He just took a deep breath, "I'm sorry to say boys, but you are not the first to find an animal in this condition. I personally have been presented with nearly a dozen this week."

"So what is doing this, Señor Espinoza?" One of the boys inquired.

"I wish I knew, at this time, your guess is as good as mine. Now be careful out there, whatever it is might be only going after small animals at the moment, but it could be a danger to humans as well, and corpses like these have been found throughout the city." The inspector warned the boys as he escorted them towards the exit. He handed the poncho to the now terrified child and closed the door tight before they could squeeze out another question.

The towering man walked back to his desk and pulled out his sketchbook and set it next to the petrified dog. It's just like all the others he had drawn before, completely drained of fluid except the bloody patch of fur over a wound on the neck.

What kind of animal could be doing this, in the middle of the city no less, and at such a scale? It didn't make sense. Perhaps a coyote, but the prey would have been consumed not drained. Whatever it was, Inspector Espinoza was quite sure he had never come across anything like it in the past.

Days passed, each with more discoveries of bled animals concentrating closer and closer to the center. The loud banging in the morning startled the sleeping inspector, and his skull awoke to a meeting with his headboard. The towering man pulled on his robe and made his way to the pounding door. Each thud pierced the newly formed lump on his crown.

He opened the door to find a frantic deputy. The officer pushed his way past the towering inspector and walked half the main room before turning to his confused host.

"It's happened, Señor Espinoza, just like you said it might. A young woman was found last night in an alley not far from the hospital. She had suffered a strange would to the neck, similar to that of the animals. And just like the others, the examiners confirmed that her body was completely depleted of blood. I think whatever you have been looking for is now coming after us."

The inspector was taken aback. He thought whatever this was would maybe be able to take down a small child, but a full-grown woman was out of the question.

This was a big move from household pets and strays. "And you say the wounds are the same."

"Come to the mortuary and see for yourself."

That's all it took to have the inspector to start getting dressed, in minutes he was grabbing his coat and sombrero and the two men were out the door. They mounted their horses and galloped in the direction of Hospital de San Miguel de Belén. A cloud was left in their wake, as the urgency of the inspector became well apparent. They reached the cemetery wall before they finally slowed to a trot. "I warn you, inspector, you will not be able to unsee what you are volunteering to witness." The inspector simply nodded, knowing very well what he was getting himself into. They dismounted and passed through the massive cast iron gate between the bricks, the mausoleum stared before them.

"This way, inspector, they have her body in the preparation room." The looming man turned and followed the constable. They followed the covered path attached to the massive fortified wall to the passageway that connects the hospital to the cemetery. "She's just through there, I'll wait for you here. I have no urge to ever see something like that again."

Inspector Espinoza entered the dawn-lit room; the covered female cadaver centered the chamber. He carefully pulled the sheet down to her clavicles; the wound on her neck was undeniably the trademark of the creature, her skin pale due to lack of blood beneath the surface. The odd thing was, like the animals, she showed no sign of scratches or marks that should be common in an animal attack. Just the lesion on her neck on an otherwise unassaulted body.

Inspector Espinoza left not being any closer to figuring out what could possibly be perpetrating these attacks. He had poured through every text he could find, but nothing matched the description. Whatever this was, no one in Guadalajara had ever seen anything like it before. The mystery consumed him. He decided to check every available avenue; if it is not an animal, then maybe he could uncover something in the more ancient texts. There has to be an explanation, and he needed to find it before anyone else was murdered.

It only took a couple of days before another body was found. Inspector Espinoza rushed to the scene of the crime. He had to know if it was the creature he was looking for. A crowd blocked the alley, but he pushed past the wall of people that separated him from the crime scene. There sprawled in the middle of the street, a man lay facedown with a gash in the base of the skull. An attack had occurred, but this was not like the others: for one, the flowerpot that had acted as the murder weapon was not but an arm's length from the victim. But Inspector Espinoza had to know for sure. "Does the body still have blood?" he asked the nearest officer.

"Ah Señor Espinoza, thinking it might be your beast, eh. Sorry, this was just your everyday gardening accident gone horribly wrong. The pot fell from just above. The Señora of the house was trying to pull a tightly rooted herb from her rooftop garden, and the thing just fell. No attack here. Hopefully, what you're looking for is gone."

A sigh of relief combined with a slight tinge of disappointment fell over the inspector. He was relieved that another person had not been attacked, but at the same time, the scene did not get him any closer to figuring out the mystery of the bloodless bodies. The man was buried the following day; the city seemed calm and perhaps free from their monster.

The day after the funeral, Inspector Espinoza decided to enter the Panteón de Belén and pay his respects to the man he had hoped was a victim to his monster. He passed through the gate and followed the covered archway to the right-hand corner where the unlucky pedestrian was buried. Espinoza was lost in his thoughts, how could he be so insensitive to be disappointed that this man was not murdered by the beast.

Then suddenly he tripped, he cursed at the annoyance of being so careless that he stumbled over a tomb or a root. He looked over to see what was the culprit that made him fall, it was him; the same man, whose grave he had come to visit, was lying just at his feet. The inspector looked to the man's burial plot, the soil was tossed in every direction. He rose to his feet to further examine the corpse; the man's neck bore the same lacerations. Espinoza pulled a knife from his side and stabbed the cadaver's arm.

The skin tore, but the blade came out clean. Just like the woman, the man had been drained of blood, but unlike her, he had already been dead and buried. Was the monster getting nervous from the hunt, or was he simply looking for the easiest prey to suckle at their jugular? The theory that he had been repressing was sharply becoming a possibility. This may actually be a vampire.

The week to come made this theory commonplace among the people of Guadalajara. Several children and another woman had fallen victim to the monster. Inspector Espinoza studied each case in great detail; he was determined to rid the city of this parasite of death. He marked the locations of each of the attacks on a map and noticed that the Panteón de Belén was at the heart of the demon's hunting territory. This is where they needed to hunt the vampire before it continued to hunt them.

He rounded up a couple deputies along with a few of his neighbors to take post around the cemetery; each man was armed with a wooden stake as goes the theory when dealing with a vampire. The sun was beginning to set, and the group had taken their place hidden upon the tombs waiting to ambush the demon. Diligent as they were, the first night still produced nothing, not even the simplest semblance of a threat. But the graveyard continued to be guarded as long as the sun did not touch the sky.

The evening had gone, and the sun was about to make its ascent, the inspector was beginning to feel the fatigue of his obsession taking its toll as the motionless night reached its end. His back was to a tree as he sat still, scanning the area in front of him when he heard the sound of dirt being kicked among the graves behind him. He slowly turned to look at the source and saw a man skulking around the graves. He continued to swipe at the ground as if he were checking the freshness of the soil.

Inspector Espinoza decided it was his duty to confront this man. He stood up and moved towards the grave surveyor, a few of the other men took notice and followed suit. Espinoza readied his stake just in case this was the demon stalking Guadalajara.

"You there, what are you doing here?" the inspector demanded as he moved closer. The man turned and glared at him. Inspector Espinoza took another step forward, and the man showed himself as a monster as he started to growl at the presence of the inspector and his men.

He was more beast than man; his demeanor was that of the other. Espinoza knew that this must be the vampire. He decided to charge, the others joined him. Together they were able to knock down the strange man, and the inspector drove his wooden stake through the man's chest. The monster had been slain, the city of Guadalajara was safe now.

They decided to bury the body immediately. The men found an empty plot and began to dig. They dug a grave twice as deep as the norm, and as they piled dirt over the vampire's body, they mixed in layers of concrete to make sure the monster stayed in its tomb.

Months later, Inspector Espinoza was on a walk and decided he would stop by the unmarked grave of the vampire that he himself had killed. He passed through the familiar iron gate, walked down the covered path along the wall to where he and his crew unceremoniously buried the beast. To his surprise, the concrete was cracked, and a seedling had made its way through.

This seedling continued to grow to enormous stature, and its roots are now beginning to occupy the neighboring graves. Many believe that this tree grew from the stake left in the vampire's heart. It is said that if you cut the tree, the tree will bleed. Rumors have circulated that late at night, you can see the faces of the vampire's victims in the grooves of its bark. The tree now is free to grow within a barrier that the government had put up to protect the tree, because the common belief is that if this tree dies, then the vampire below will awaken.

Whether or not Inspector Espinoza actually killed a vampire that night is still uncertain. No one has dared to unearth the tree to see what lies beneath. This tree stands as a marker to the evil that resides in the Panteón de Belén, where we will remain to witness our next story.

By this point, Catholicism is the prevalent religion and has become integral in the lives of the people of México. It is still the latter part of the nineteenth century when we meet our next guest of Belén. A child with a grave illness was challenging to help during this time; in the 1800s, his illness was beyond even the greatest minds in the medical field.

This young boy had his faith challenged by his condition. And who can blame him for questioning a higher power, when he was suffering a pain than what should ever be burdened by a child. We enter the hospital attached to the cemetery to watch the battle of…

SANTIAGO VS GOD

Young Santiago's illness had grown worse, and he was forced to take up residence in the Hospital de San Miguel de Belén. The pain in his stomach had become too harsh to carry out simple tasks, sometimes even getting up to walk was too much torment for him to stand. All he wanted was to play like the other kids his age, but he was confined to his bed to battle this horrific cancer that tore at his insides.

His mother would spend day and night at his side, encouraging him; her desire for him to live was probably why he had lived this long with the ailment. But the pain only increased as time passed and the doctors had run out of ways to help. His mother's faith was becoming not enough. She would kneel at his bedside and into her clasped hands plea, bargain, and praise God in the firm belief that the Lord would deliver a response.

His condition worsened each day, death was certain to come to Santiago unless God decided to intervene. One night the pain hit its pinnacle. His mother had carried with her a picture of Santiago's favorite Saint, who happened to hold the same name. The Paton Saint of Spanish pilgrims had always been Santiago's protector, and he needed Him now more than ever. The boy eventually succumbed to the pain and lost consciousness. His mother placed the paper saint in his palms. He tightened his grip, but his eyes remained clenched shut.

Hours passed before the demon inside him forced his eyes open again. Santiago turned fetal, pulling his arms to his chest as he rolled to his side.

Through searing tears, he noticed the card in his hands. He raised the photo closer to see the saint looking down at him. His guardian mocked him from above, no intent to save him from this agony. Santiago pulled the card to his chest and stared at the Saint's picture, drops of resentment wetted its surface. The image sparked a flame of anger in the boy, and he threw it to the ground.

His mother jumped up from her slumber in the chair to attend to her son. "What's wrong, my boy? What can I do to help?"

Santiago was not ready to deal with another person, as his most painful nerve endings were being attacked and consumed by the monster inside of his stomach. He just wanted to be alone. Nothing was going to make him feel better. The pain traveled through his body. He was possessed, and the demon was in the most rigorous part of its torture. Santiago could only muster out gasps and grunts.

His mother hit her knees and began to pray. "Oh, Lord, please spare my son. We pray to you, Heavenly Father, ease my boy's pain." Her eyes remained fixated on the concrete ceiling above. "We believe in you, Jesus Christ, Dear Maria, show us your grace." Santiago watched with pity as his mother begged the walls for salvation.

"Oh God, my only God, show mercy. We believe and are your humble servants. Lord, we love you." God was not going to help, and Santiago didn't want his mother to gravel for his graciousness.

"Get out! I'm sorry, mom, but you have to leave. I need to be alone tonight. Just go. I'll see you in the morning."

Startled by her son's request, she rose from her knees and collected her things. She attempted a reply, but each was caught in a sniffle and reduced to barely a sound. She followed Santiago's request and left the room. She composed herself and went home for a well-deserved rest. She would return to her boy bright and early in the morning. He is safe under the care of the doctors and nurses, and a good night's sleep would do her wonders.

Santiago glared at this God on the ceiling that his mother insisted on giving praise. The ceiling did nothing. God was not coming. This God that he had been taught to love with the promise of reciprocation was never showing. He was not here to take away the pain; He had left Santiago there to suffer. Santiago felt betrayed.

"Where are you, God? Why have you done this to me? What did I do wrong, or do you just hate children? I bet if you had this sickness, you wouldn't give it to kids. I wish you had this. I wish you could feel the pain that I feel. I wish you could suffer like I am. I hate you. I hate you for doing this to me. What kind of God does this to His people? If you were sick like me, then you would understand. I want you to hurt. You wouldn't do this if you knew what it was like. You should have this, not me!"

Members of the staff shuddered as the boy continued to curse God. Some began to believe that it must be the devil that made this boy ill, and an exorcism would be the only cure. The judgmental eyes watching him from afar did not deter Santiago's conviction that God deserved his pain. He continued to shout at the God who abandoned him deep into the late hours of the night.

A shriek acted as the morning crow and startled the residents of the Hospital de San Miguel de Belén. Staff converged on the cemetery to inquire into what was causing this premature disturbance. They were not prepared for the terror they were about to see. One by one, they congregated to witness the unsightly horror outside.

The body of a boy swayed from the lower branch of the tree standing outside of an open patient's window. A noose crafted from hospital bed sheets prevented his lifeless body from touching the ground. The linen strangled child was finally free from the suffering he endured from the room on the other side of the open window. Santiago had ended his argument with God.

A few weeks later, the previously healthy tree gave way to rot. The groundsman was forced to cut it down to a stump. But in this cemetery, a tree is not to be left alone from the supernatural. Every evening when the light shines in just the right direction, this stump casts a shadow of a full tree with a small body hanging from its lower branch. Santiago escaped his disease, but he will never be able to escape Belén.

Parents tell this story to their children to show them the repercussions of blasphemy. Whether God punished this child for cursing His name or a staff member killed him for the same reason or poor Santiago simply took his own life to escape the pain, one cannot say. But the coincidence that this happened in the same cemetery that housed a vampire is not lost on me and only adds to the intrigue of this potentially haunted place.

We leave the cemetery and head north to the desert. We arrive in the city of Durango, a town known for one thing: scorpions. Here we meet a man who has found himself captured by a corrupt system that has bent the law to appease a wealthy landowner.

Corruption in the police force is widespread in México and...

David Zelnar

I JUST JUAN TO BE FREE

"Wait, wait! I'm not supposed to be here. There's been some sort of mistake. I'm not supposed to be here." Juan flailed as he resisted being put into a cell.

"Quiet you, this is exactly where you belong." The guard shoved Juan onto the dusty cement and slammed the bars closed behind him. "This is your home now, you better get used to it." The man stated as he left the new prisoner to gather his bearings.

Juan stammered to the back of the cage, and his new roommates watched as the panic-stricken man pinned himself against the solid wall. He arched his back against the concrete and filled his chest with air. A long exhale, and his head popped back to life. "Hi, I'm Juan, how are you?" With a smile on his face, he greeted the three men with whom he was to share his current domicile.

"Are you guys all from Durango?" One thing about Juan was no matter how dire the circumstances may be, he always found a way to recuperate and maintain his genuinely happy and endearing demeanor. Two of his cellmates nodded, but one simply murmured Jalisco. "Ah, I've never been, but it sounds lovely. How could the birthplace of tequila not be?" The man just scoffed and rolled over in his bunk.

"It's a shame to be confined like this. The animals on the ranch had more freedom than we do in this tiny cage. This is less than human." Juan continued to break the ice.

"Well, you better get used to it. This is where they send those not fit for society," the older prisoner sitting across from where Juan was standing responded. "Say, what gets a nice fella like you thrown in here with the likes of us anyway?"

Juan took a step back, "How do you mean Señor?"

"Well, I'm the town drunk, Diego. Fernando here is a bandito, and Hector over there, well Hector shot a man and then fled Jalisco." The funny man callously replied.

"But that is just the thing Señor, I didn't do anything. I am not supposed to be here. I am being accused of something I most certainly did not do."

"Well, someone sure as hell thinks you did," spat Fernando.

Diego became intrigued. "So say then, what are they saying you did?"

"They are calling me a thief."

"And what might they believe you have stolen?" Fernando asked as he leaned forward.

"See, that's not even the point. I've been framed to have my love taken from me.

This is just a ploy to keep me out of the way so that he can court Lupe. While I am locked away in here, he will do everything in his power to win her hand. He is as persistent as he is evil. A lamb has been left under the eye of a coyote." Juan began rambling off to himself about conspiracies and such.

Then he steered the conversation in another direction, "Hey! You guys want to play a game? I always keep a deck of cards in my vest pocket, and I know a game that might just make this place a little more bearable." The fellow prisoners joined Juan in a makeshift circle in the area between the two bunk beds, even Hector showed interest in doing something other than wait and sleep.

"Ok, so here is how the game goes. Each of us gets four cards that we are not allowed to look at, and here is a draw pile. We each take turns drawing cards and decide whether to use them or change them for the ones we already have. The lowest amount of points win. Deuce through ten are worth their number, face cards are worth ten, well except the suicide king and the man with the axe, they are worth minus one, and jokers are worth zero. Aces, of course, are worth one. Ya with me?"

The men half-nodded, and Juan continued, "Ok, so if you draw a seven or eight, then you can look at one of your own cards. If you draw a nine or ten, then you can look at someone else's card. Red jacks and queens mean you can look at someone else's card and change it for your own, but black ones mean that you can still change, but you can't look. When you think you have the lowest score, say 'Cambio,' and everyone gets one last turn to get their score lower than yours without touching your cards. Oh, let's just play, and you'll get it as we go along."

Everyone shrugged their shoulders and began to play. "Ok, you get one look at your bottom two cards and then no looking after." They all peaked three or four times to make sure they had the cards memorized. A few rounds go by, and they start to pick up the rules. Hector calls "Cambio," and the players reveal their total, Juan looked at Hector with hesitation. "Hector,

I'm so sorry, but the black kings are worth ten points, and you have two." Hector furrowed his brow in annoyed confusion. "But hey, let's reshuffle and play again. That's the glory of this game; as soon as one game is finished, a new one can begin." Juan quickly dealt new cards to his cellmates.

After a few hands and a basic understanding of the game, Diego decided to pry further into the odd young man's incarceration. "So, Juan. You said earlier that it didn't really matter what they said you took, to me that sounds more like it matters more who is saying you took it, am I right?" Juan sighed. Diego pressed on, "Why don't you tell us what happened. We're all mighty curious how a nice boy like you could end up in a place like this. So do tell us, won't you?"

"Well, it all began a few months ago when the Rodriguez's niece, Lupe, had moved to town. Oh, what a sight, no man in all of Durango had seen a woman of such beauty. She brought with her the spring air. I swear to you flowers would go into bloom as she would pass."

"Alright, alright. She was pretty; we get it. But still doesn't explain why you're here." Fernando growled.

Hector shushed him, "He's gettin' to it. You got somewhere else you got to be?"

Juan continued, "Right, so at that time, I was a ranch hand for the Ortiz family, and I was smitten by this girl. I would plan my day and go out of my way so we could 'bump' into each other. And those times that we did, oh it was magic, I tell you. In no time, we were certain that the stars had aligned to bring us together. You could not find a better match. But soon, it became apparent that the recently widowed Señor Ortiz also had his eye on the lovely Lupe. He had made several advances towards the less than intrigued woman, but her dismissions only fed the flame of his persistence. When he found out about Lupe and I's affair, he became bewildered with jealousy and claimed that I stole from his study. Without hesitation, the sheriff arrested me and tossed me in here with you lot. No real charges and no idea of how long I am to remain behind bars, my fate lies in the hands of the monster who cast me here in the first place."

A disappointed groan was heard from down the hall. A young guard with the beginnings of a prominent mustache in his future approached the cell. "Is that true? Are you really only in here to help old man Ortiz prey upon that girl? That can't be right. Hold on, I'm going to sort this out." Before Juan could answer one of his questions, the guard was gone, and the jail was left without a chaperone.

The door was locked, and a gunshot was usually the reward for an escape without a plan, so the men continued their game. A dozen or so hands later, the guard returned with the same concerned look on his face. "You truly upset a powerful and fiendish man. He plans to keep you in here indefinitely until his people can conclude their 'investigation' into what you procured from the ranch. This is to assist in our prosecution. Honest to God, his words."

Juan tossed his cards onto the pile. "How can you just allow this?"

"Señor, there is more. I told him of your feelings towards this girl and how you stated that it was fate that you were together." The guard hesitated.

"And? Tell me, did you seal my fate to living in this cell forever? What did he say?"

"Señor, his request is beyond reason."

"What is it?" Juan pleaded.

The guard cleared his throat and composed himself, "He said, 'that if it was truly fate that you are supposed to be with this girl, then fate would protect you from the Célula de la Muerte.' He said that if you spend a night in the Cell of Death and survive, then fate truly wants you two together, and he will drop all of the charges against you, and you will be freed. But I'm telling you, you do not want to do this suicidal task. I have worked in this jail for three years now, and not one man who has spent the night in that cell has left alive. There is a curse upon that cell, and it is not to be taken lightly. Do not accept his terms."

"But what choice do I have?" Juan queried through the bars. "He could keep me here forever, and my dear Lupe is not safe with that devil hiding in the shadows. Take me to this cell. I fear no curse. All I ask for is a handful of candles and a book of matches. I will face your phantom and wake to my freedom. I accept his terms." Juan stood tall like a torero before the carnage.

The guard slowly turned the key in the lock, he sighed as if he was preparing a man for his unrightful execution. He wanted to try and change his prisoner's mind, but the look of resolution on Juan's face quickly deterred him. He escorted the man to the last cell in the hall. It was barely big enough to fit a single person; a metal door had replaced the bars. Its position eluded the sun, making it cooler than the other cells. The chill created an unsettling dampness in the air of the small room. The sun was just beginning to set, and yet the cell afforded barely a hint of light.

Juan sat down on the bare floor, and the guard handed him five thin candles and a nearly fresh book of matches. The guard looked at Juan with pity; he was certain he would be removing his corpse in the morning. Juan looked up with a grin and held up his flammable light sources with confidence. He nodded in assurance, and his hat fell forward over his eyes. The door closed, and darkness consumed all that lay beyond the brim of his headwear. His hand became a barely recognizable blur waving just inches in front of his face. His candles would be his only reprieves from this darkness, so he lit one to get his bearings.

The glow bounced around the bare room, a simple cot and Juan were its only occupants. He moved over to the bed and prepared himself for sleep. There is no worry in sleep. He lied down but kept the lit candle sitting on his chest. The wax was already nearing its bottom third.

Juan blew it out to preserve the time he could escape the darkness in the future.

He stared at the immeasurable ceiling then closed his eyes, thinking of the brightness of his freedom just hours away. These men must just be a fable to scare people from going to jail; this is just a cell like any other. He nuzzled in and let thoughts of Lupe carry him to sleep. Dreams were beginning to take shape when scratching across the concrete brought Juan back to our reality. He franticly struck a match and pulled one of the full candles from his side to its flame. The scratching moved in quick steps and echoed from the other corner along the back wall, but the light from the torch was not fast enough to catch its source. He waved the candle back and forth, but the sound seeped into the wall and disappeared.

Juan decided that he must have dreamed this sound, that it was just his mind playing tricks on him. But no matter, the haunting scratch-tap chewed at his eardrums and sleep was no longer an option. He positioned himself on his knees, his candles and matches to his front: Juan was in battle position. He set the candle on the floor to burn to its end. Three and a third left; how these candles burned quickly.

It wasn't long after the embers died did the scratch-tap return. It moved slowly this time, uniformed steps overlapping each other. The unnatural sound of its feet striking the pavement ticked as if it lacked padding. The creature marched towards the cot, but Juan managed to light a candle and wield it at his assailant. The scratching quickened its pace but in the opposite direction. Juan peered beyond his miniature torch and saw the most massive scorpion he had ever seen, glaring at him from across the room.

He had lived in Durango his entire life and was used to scorpions, but he had never come across one like this. It was menacing with its magnificent pincers as its enormous tail quivered with venom.

Juan quickly realized that the scorpion feared the flame from his candle. All he had to do was keep the candles lit, and the monstrous arachnid would keep its distance, but this candle was already halfway gone. He pushed the flame closer, but the creature seemed to find comfort at its range and simply focused on its prey. Juan grabbed another full candle since the one in his hand was nearing its end. Nothing could explain why in this dark, cool place, the candles seemed to melt like they were trying to brighten the desert sky at high noon. Juan was now down to one and a third with only a handful of matches, and the scorpion did not look like it was losing patience.

He saw his hat and tossed it onto the scorpion like he was playing a game of ring toss. The hat barely covered the creature, and the darkness gave it newfound confidence. It started to walk forward. Juan leaped forward to keep the danger under the crown of his hat and not on the loose trying to sting him, but the sudden movement extinguished his flame. He scrambled around and found the matches and relit his life source. The hat was flat, and the scorpion was nowhere to be seen. He grabbed the last third of a candle and lit it with the remains of his last full one. Scratches came at every flicker.

Juan pulled out the matchbook and exposed the sticks for ignition. The candle faded into its wax, and the scorpion charged its target that was now in its element. Juan focused. The movement was coming from 10:30; he struck the matchbook against the concrete and slid the enflamed box in that direction. The fire skipped through the darkness and exposed a fleeing arachnid. Juan ran over and covered the creature while its stinger was turned. He pressed the brim tightly to the ground as the enraged scorpion continually pierced the sides of the crown. Juan held the hat firmer to the ground until the animal lost vigor and became still. He must remain diligent in this task; he would keep this monster in its trap until the sun had come to rise, however long that may be.

He was surprised when the door opened moments shortly after. The guard stepped in and, to his delight, saw that the prisoner had not perished in the Cell of Death. He reached his hand out to help the man squatting over his hat to his freedom.

"I can't." Juan snapped. "It's under here. It was a giant scorpion that had been killing all of those prisoners, and I have it here under my hat. You need to get something to kill it quickly!"

The guard pulled around his rifle, "I could shoot it," he suggested.

"Are you mad? If you miss, it could get away, or worse yet, you could shoot me, and then I get stung." Juan declared. "No, no, no. We need to stab it or something."

The guard stepped on Juan's hands, "Say goodbye to your sombrero Señor." He pointed the barrel to the top and pushed it down until he could feel the only thing keeping his gun from the scorpion was the material of this hat. Juan slid his hands out from under the guard's feet, which had now taken over their role in holding down the brim. Juan put his fingers in his ears as the guard pulled the trigger.

The room filled with dust and a deafening ring. The two men waved to clear the vision of their target. Did they kill it, or was it still on the loose hidden in the sediment? Nothing else mattered. The guard used the barrel of his gun to lift what was left of Juan's hat. To their relief, the shrapnel filled carcass of the scorpion lay underneath. The cell was free of its phantom.

Then it dawned on Juan, he was a free man now. The guard understood immediately and pointed towards the door. Juan, his head still ringing from the gun going off in such small quarters and close proximity, tried to wipe the dust from his eyes to better his burning sight as he stumbled towards the exit of the jail. He could hear the faint cheers of his roommates as he passed but continued to walk as he tried to clear his vision. He made it to the front door and squinted through his tear-filled eyes to find Lupe waiting for him at the entrance. The stars must have remained aligned.

From time to time, a story does have a happy ending. Though Juan and Lupe were still left to a world where the wealthy hold influence even over those who have sworn an oath to protect the citizens. Greed demeans the character of the soul and can push a person to hold monetary gains over the life of a human being. The police in this story are as much to blame as the petty landowner, who only flexed the power allotted him.

We head back south to the state of Jalisco, but we are going to pass by Guadalajara at the moment and head down to the small town of Lagos de Moreno. Here we will meet a candy storeowner whose family has left him to himself in his old age. As time passed, they deserted their patriarch who just needed...

A
LITTLE
HELP

Nested on a small avenue where the bees had come to reclaim their sugar laid a shop of the most delectable treats. The buzzing hovered over the candied tamarind, sweet potatoes, nuts, mangos, and other colorful fruits that lined the entrance to the piles of palanquetas, marzipans, every delicious mix of dulce de leche one could think of, fruit gummies wrapped in chili powder, coconut bars, both sweet and spicy lollipops, wafers, cocadas and serpentinas, spoon suckers, sweet bars with varieties of nuts and seed, not to mention the special candies for that season.

This house-sized piñata belonged to Francisco Pérez, more affectionately known by the locals of his neighborhood as Don Pancho. His candies were the finest in the area, and no one could contest his sugary crown.

One day while peeling tamarind pods, an unexpected visitor greeted Pancho. The scent of the ripened fruit had gained the curiosity of a little brown mouse. Little by little, it shuffled closer to the candy man, distancing itself from the security of its hole it had so precisely chewed through the baseboard along the wooden wall. The mouse looked up at the aging sugar connoisseur curiously, Pancho smiled and held out an already candied piece of fruit for his newly introduced houseguest. The rodent hesitated at first but then snatched the candy and scurried a few feet away for insurance that the candy was indeed a gift. The mouse made a little squeak and then ran back into the wall. Pancho continued shucking away for his next batch of tamarind candies.

The next day the new little visitor returned while Pancho was caramelizing peanuts early in the morning. It ran up to about four floor tiles from the candy maker and sat back on its hind legs.

Its head mimicked the movement of the pan in Pancho's hand, a repetitive nod to every flip of the glazed legumes. The scent from the sugar cooking onto the bouncing nuts entranced the little creature. Pancho looked over his shoulder and popped one of the steaming treats from the pan. The mouse scurried forward and patted at the hot morsel. Once it was cool enough, the tiny guest quickly devoured his treat.

This became a daily routine between the candy maker and his little tenant. The mouse would dance and pirouette to the candy man's delight, who in return treated the critter to ever essence he could find in the market, taking note of his new friend's preferences. The company brought newfound life to the old man; the amusement of watching his pintsized taste tester brought him deeper into the bazar than he had ever gone in his youth. He was producing flavors that he had never dared to turn into confections before.

The two companions enjoyed their sugar-dusted camaraderie for quite some time before the candy maker took ill. The sickness made the task of running the candy shop tiresome for the elderly man, and eventually, it became too difficult. This increased the strain of paying for the doctor's twice a week visits along with the cost of medicine. Although his funds were diminishing, he continued to share his daily meal with the mouse. Food was running out, but his little friend never felt the consequences.

The food stocks had reached about a two-day ration, and there was no more money to replenish even the basics. Pancho sighed in his favorite chair as he stared at the mechanisms he longed to operate again. What was he to do if he ran out of food? He had sent word to his daughters but never received a reply.

The little mouse again made his daily appearance but was confused by his typically jolly amigo's defeated demeanor. It cocked its head side to side, studying the candy maker. It glanced at the crumbles on the plate then sat still as if in deep thought. Its eyes bounced, nose twitched, ears flickered; the tiny brown rodent turned and hurried back to its hole in the floorboard. Pancho watched at the mouse's odd behavior and leaned towards its domicile. Seconds later, it reemerged from its dwelling with a silver coin grasped in its hands. It was enough to buy groceries for a week. Pancho couldn't believe his luck of having this little lifesaving compatriot.

Every time the pantry would get low, the mouse would return with another coin to buy more. The man no longer had to fear hunger along with his sickness. The mouse continued to finance their rations for several more weeks, but even this miracle was not enough to stifle the illness, and Pancho's ailments worsened. It wasn't until the old man was facing death that his granddaughters finally came to visit the poor dying Francisco, eldest of the Pérez line.

The last thing Don Pancho asked the girls to do was to watch over the little mouse and to make sure that it was housed and fed. He told them of what his little friend had done for him when he needed it the most. Francisco Pérez passed shortly thereafter and was given a small service.

It did not take long after the funeral for the granddaughters to return to Pancho's home and shop to handle the mouse. The girls entered the kitchen and grabbed some wedging tools. They charged towards the wall with the hole. They began prying the panels away; the search for the mouse's horde of treasure began. Pancho's granddaughters peeled every strip of the walling from the home; but to no avail, not a coin or mouse was found, just destruction of the home Pancho so dearly loved. They were covered in dust from the ruins of their grandfather's life's work.

Hidden away, the little brown mouse watched the greed-consumed girls destroy the candy maker's home. It made its way to the door left ajar by the hasty treasure hunters. The mouse took one last look with pity its eyes and departed never to be seen again.

The only thing that can destroy a person worse than greed is fear. Phobias can debilitate the mind, and irrationally consume the conscience. The boy we will meet next proves just that.

We head back to Guadalajara. It is May 24th, 1882, and the weather is beginning to drift to the rainy season. The sun has set over a tiny family home. The parents are putting their little boy to bed, and every night he asks his mother, "Please...

David Zelnar

KEEP ME IN THE LIGHT

The wind was beginning to rustle the trees, clouds had converged over the city; a great storm was on its way. Little Ignacio's parents were putting their frightened child to sleep. The boy was not afraid of the tempest or the constant flashes of lightning that it would bring. Ignacio, or Nachito as his parents liked to call him, was afraid of the dark. Since he could remember, his parents had always made sure to light two torches by his open window, so that way, he would never be left to suffer in the darkness; but this storm threatened to extinguish this comfort.

"Oh, Nachito, don't you worry. We will not let anything hurt you; there is nothing to fear. The world is still the same, whether it be lit by the sun or consumed by the night. We are here, and we will protect you." His mother reassured him before closing his bedroom door.

The young boy took a deep breath. She was right; as long as he was in his home, there was no reason to be afraid. The torches were showing resilience against the wind, and his family was nearby to ward off any dangers. His nerves began to ease, but the howls and booms of the storm continued to make their presence known. Ignacio pulled the sheet to his chin. If I fall asleep now, then I will wake to the brightness of the sun. He squeezed his eyes shut and thought of the day to come.

Thunder continued to crash, keeping the child from entering his dreams. The wind danced with his curtains and tested the fortitude of the torches. The barely flickering light threatened to be smothered by the shadows. Each gust put the flames in peril. Little Nachito's soul would go tense as the wicks battled the elements struggling to reignite. He knew that it would not be long before the storm took his light away.

The gales carried the voices of the spirits to

Ignacio's window. They were calling for him to join them in the darkness. The waning flashes of flame were his sole safeguards against the wraiths entering his room. He feared that he would not survive the night if they were to be extinguished. The darkness swam with evil, and Nachito's lifeboat was threatening to capsize.

The footsteps of God boomed through the storm as He marched towards Ignacio's window. The spirits' howls chased His stride. Flashes of souls meeting their end accompanied the madness of the tempest. Nachito knew it was but a matter of time before the flames would falter, and he would be left unprotected with the curse of blindness.

Scratching of claws like branches against siding begged to enter the frame of his window. The yearning shrieks of the spirits swirled at the threshold. The protective flames were ultimately defeated in their effort to illuminate Ignacio from the evil at his door. All light drifted away, and Nachito floated in a sea of darkness, susceptible to what lay beyond his limited sight.

The room fell into nothing. The noises climbed their way into the bedroom, hiding in the corners when the sky would crack in angst. Nothing was there to keep the darkness away except the exploding lights coming from above. Nachito sunk into his blankets, it was but a soft barricade between him and the spirits. He began to shake; each sound could be his last. His heart quickened pace as the strikes became less frequent, giving the night longer reign over the room. He waited for a creature to appear in every flash. But the lightning faded and the clouds opened to rain.

The sounds of freefalling balls of water's impact against concrete flooded the room consumed in total blackness. Nachito could not see his hands. He was beginning to disappear into the darkness. It was too dark. It shouldn't be this dark. Terror set in; Ignacio's nine-year-old brain could not focus on anything but the blackness. His breath became shallow, and his heart continued to panic. His eyes were no longer useful to the blind. Would they ever be again? His breathing quickened; anxiety squeezed him from inside. A ringing replaced the rain. He inhaled twice to every exhale. Then everything went black.

The next morning Ignacio's parents entered his room to check on their child.   They slid his blanket from his loose grip clenched above his temple, revealing a face frozen in a permanent state of fright.   Fear had stolen his pigment and left the empty vessel of a boy cemented in terror. His mother pulled at his lifeless body, pleading to God in desperation, but the boy remained still.

The tale of the child's death spread through the neighborhood, every family having their own take on the cause.   The funeral at the Panteón de Belén was fraught with spectators vulturing over the mourning family.   It was a heart attack; it was a ghost; it was God: whispers filled the atmosphere of the somber event.   A spectacle of mystery in a time of assured routine.   The child was interred, and, one by one, the bystanders dispersed, eventually leaving only the mother to say goodbye to her Nachito.

The next morning she decided she had to return and see her baby.   She passed through the cast-iron gate, followed the covered path, and quickly approached her son's grave.   To her disgust, she discovered his resting place had been disturbed, and Nachito's casket lay next to the hole where it was laid to rest the day before.   "What kind of disturbingly grotesque person could dig up a child?" She thought. The weeping mother crawled to her son's coffin; it looked just as it did when it was buried.

She forced open the lid to see Ignacio undisturbed other than the permanently petrified expression on his face.

One of the groundsmen found the distraught woman screaming for answers and saw the open casket by her side. He retrieved more assistance, and the cemetery's employees consoled the woman and began digging to rebury the poor, unearthed child. Her husband was tracked down, and he rushed to rescue his wife from the horrendous scene and bring her home. She continued to desperately question, "Why was he out of the ground? What did they want? Who would disturb a child's grave?" Ignacio's father sank as he was unable to give the woman he loved an explanation. She spent the rest of the evening leaning over a candle staring out the window at the darkness.

Upon the rising of the sun, she was drawn to the Panteón de Belén once again. She had to make sure her son was all right, even in death. But once again she arrived to the same scene. The casket was out of the ground, yet undisturbed. Why is this happening? What have I done to deserve this? Her mind was set that someone was out to cause her harm, and it was working.

They buried the boy once again, but the casket continued to rise from the earth. This pattern sustained for another nine days straight. No one could figure out why this was happening. It became a case for the entire neighborhood. Yet, no solution had any impact on keeping the boy in the ground overnight.

Then it dawned on Ignacio's mother what was disturbing her child. He was still afraid of the dark; they needed to make a grave above the ground so her Nachito could see the light.

They built the boy a coffin made from stone and set it upon four pillars to elevate it above the ground. The new tomb remains undisturbed to this day. But many people believe they have seen the spirit of Nachito in or near the cemetery. They say they either see a boy or see balloons floating at a child's height alone. Today his grave is continually adorned with offerings of toys for the spirit of little Ignacio; some believe he will grant a favor in return. The holidays bring an abundance of sacramental toys and stuffed animals for Nachito, the caretakers of the cemetery donate them to local hospitals for their ill children. Ignacio's death remains the talk of the neighborhood.

We finish our journey through the tales of México with one of the most famous stories of all. Few love stories become that of legend. The fated couple we are about to meet transcends any work of fiction.

This story does not just take place in a single location and takes many years to culminate. We begin our journey at the turn of the twentieth century. A young artist is just starting his career, unaware that fate has put him on a path that will lead to...

A
MEETING
FOR
500 PESOS

From time to time, a chance meeting completely diverts a life's course. In this case, the crossing of these two dynamic souls' paths redirected history.

Diego Rivera showed great promise as an artist beginning at a young age. At the age of twenty-one, he was sponsored by the Governor of Veracruz to study art in Spain. He shortly after moving to Paris to work and paint. He was living during the birth of Cubism and followed his contemporaries in this style until he came across the paintings of Cezanne and transformed his style to more simplistic figures with brighter colors. He had found his style that would remain in the minds of generations to come.

This time in Paris was when he met the Russian artist Angelina Beloff, and it did not take long for the two to fall in love and marry. Their marriage was hit with many tribulations. The First World War put dire financial stress on those in the art community, making it difficult to purchase the necessary supplies. Angelina decided to put Diego's artistic career ahead of her own, she worked and supported him as his art began to gain notoriety.

Things only became more difficult when the two had a son who was not long for this world. At a little over a year old, the child died of lung complications. Diego only added more strife to the relationship siring a daughter with another woman shortly after. The two remained together through these hardships, for Angelina truly believed in his work.

When Diego was thirty-four, he decided to travel through Italy to gain a better perspective of the Renaissance painters. Upon returning to France, he was asked to come back to México by the Minister of Education to be involved in a government-sponsored mural program following the Mexican revolution. Still stricken by poverty, the couple could only afford to send Diego on this voyage. He never returned to Angelina.

It did not take long for Diego to start romantically pursuing another woman after returning to México. Within a year of his reunion with his home country, he married the model and novelist Guadalupe Marin. She was there to accompany him as an assistant and model for his first government-sponsored mural at the National Preparatory School in México City. Here he was going to experiment in encaustic, the mixing of pigment and beeswax for his first significant mural, *Creation*.

Frida Kahlo was one of only a handful of female students admitted to the National Preparatory School in México City. She was focusing on the natural sciences with hopes of becoming a doctor, due to her own battles with Polio as a child. The disease had left her with a limp but had no effect on her spirit.

Frida had a history of being disobedient, being expelled from a previous school for being insubordinate, but her academic prowess gained her admittance into this elite institution. She had formed an informal rebellious Communist group called the Cachuchas. They would pull pranks, fight against conservatism, perform dissident plays, and openly debate philosophy and politics with their peers. Many members of this group grew up to become the Mexican intelligentsia.

Diego was painting his mural the first time he encountered Frida's voice. She had snuck into the Bolivar Auditorium and hid behind one of the great columns. She peeked from her hiding space and saw the portly artist hard at work, mixing color into the wax, preparing to bring his next figure to life.

She smirked and shouted into the unoccupied hall to distract the preoccupied artist, "You better watch out Diego! Nahui is coming!"

Diego turned and looked out into the empty auditorium. He cocked his head at the peculiar heckle and then returned to his work, but this voice reverberated in his mind. It was several nights before it would reintroduce itself in the flesh.

Rivera was up on the scaffolding while his wife was busy assisting below. Voices of students bounced off the large wooden doors that provided an entrance to the auditorium. The commotion outside continued to intensify as the doors began to heave like a lung struggling to breathe, occasionally coughing out loud echoing bangs. The entrance's respiration quickened as if it was gasping for air until like an explosion, the doors burst open.

A mob of students stumbled through, at the front, a young Frida, her hair falling over her face. She pulled back her bangs, and as she looked up, she locked eyes with the muralist. A youthful face, but oddly dignified. Deep eyes veiled by thick eyebrows gave this newly developed girl the poise of a woman.

She stepped forward from the stumbling students behind her and earnestly requested, "Would it be of any nuisance if I watched you work?"

Diego turned on the scaffold with one hand on his pistol that he kept in case of threatening right-wing students. "Of course not my dear, it would be my pleasure."

Frida walked to the front row to get optimal observation of the work being shaped and sat down, the other students dispersed in the background. Her eyes focused on the painter. She followed his every movement, his every stroke. As paint became creation, her world transformed into pigment growing on walls.

Nothing else seemed to exist. Each brush reshaped reality.

Guadalupe scoffed at this young girl so fixated upon her husband. She would glare at the child, but Frida's eyes never averted from the artist's movement. "What a strange girl this is," she mocked to her husband. "Just sitting there staring at you like a child possessed." Diego chuckled at his wife's jealousy of the adolescent.

This furthered Guadalupe's anger at this insolent child captivated by her husband. She decided it was time to scare this star-struck pest from her perch. She stomped over to Frida and with hands on her hips bent at the waist to the point that her nose threatened to collide with Frida's. "What an odd little thing you are. Just sitting here staring like a moth to a light. Shouldn't you be running around being a student and not pestering artists as they work with your incessant hovering? This is not a normal thing for you to be doing."

Frida simply met Guadalupe's stare and unnervingly reciprocated the glare without showing much concern for this woman berating her. She looked straight through her, not letting her eyes distract from anything but this woman's pupils. Guadalupe flinched first, smiled, and then marched up to her husband on the scaffold.

"Look at this girl, as small as she is, she is not intimidated by a tall, strong woman such as myself. I think I like her."

Frida stayed in the same position observing the muralist paint for a few more hours. Still, she never moved, her eyes forever locked on the creation of the masterpiece. Then suddenly she stood up, said good night and left, not to be seen by Diego for years to come. He learned about a year later the name of this young girl from the director who complained that it was because of this Frida Kahlo and her misfit friends that he was considering resigning.

Frida continued working towards becoming a doctor, but her dream came crashing down in an instant when she was just eighteen. On their way home from school, Frida and her then-boyfriend, a fellow Cachucha, were riding in a wooden bus on their way across town when it collided with a streetcar. The accident killed several people and nearly took Frida's life as well. The impact broke her ribs, collarbone, and both of her legs. During the crash, a handrail came loose, impaled Frida in the pelvis, fractured her pelvic bone, and displaced three of her vertebrates.

Kahlo was confined to her bed in a plaster corset for the better part of two years after leaving the hospital. The isolation left Frida to her thoughts, and she had to find a release from the solitary confinements of her mind. Frida had an easel rigged so that she could paint in bed. She attached a mirror to the top to begin practicing self-portraits. In this time, she painted mostly herself, her sisters, and images she could procure of her classmates. She wanted to paint them in the way she saw them and only the way she envisioned them in reality.

She was already twenty by the time she was able to reunite with her friends. By this time, they had already begun university, and Frida was well behind. She quickly joined the Mexican Communist Party and met activists, artists, and the occasional political exile. She learned from a member of her group that Diego Rivera was painting a fresco at the Ministry of Education and decided he could help her determine her future.

Diego was in the midst of painting from the scaffolding when a familiar sound came from below. He looked down at the petite young woman with her thick signature eyebrows staring up at him. "Diego, will you please come down? I have something important to discuss with you."

Without even recognizing who was making this demand, he obliged and started making his way down the scaffolding. Instinct sent him to comply with this sound indistinctly coming from his memory.

"Now, I am not here for fun. I need to make a living, and I have made some paintings that I would like you to look at as a professional. I want your opinion on whether I have the potential to make a career as an artist or if I am just self-indulging my own vanity. I have brought three with me. Will you come and take a look at them?"

Rivera stepped onto the pavement and agreed to look at the young woman's paintings. He followed her to a cubicle under a staircase where she had stored her work. She turned each of her paintings to face Diego. Each one was a portrait of a woman. Diego's eyes widened as the impressive work revealed itself. The images were honest and not overly original, as many young artists try to make in a vain mistake of trying to be unique. The work displayed the necessary sensuality cast by a genuine and realist observer. Flaws were shown, and the beauty accentuated but without losing the humanity of the subject. This girl was a true artist in his eyes.

Frida noticed the enthusiasm on Diego's face and pursed her lips. She was well aware of his womanizing past and was not here in pursuit of underhanded flattery. "Now I have not come here looking for compliments. I want the honest criticism of a professional. I am not an art lover or an amateur. I am simply a girl who must make a living."

He eyed the portraits once again. Squatting as he inched closer to inspect the detail of her brushstrokes and then stepping back to see the full perspective of the piece. After going back and forth between the trio, Diego responded, "In my opinion, no matter how difficult it is for you, you must continue to paint."

"Ok then, I will do that. I have one more favor to ask of you as a professional. Sunday, will you come to my place to see the rest of my work?" Diego quickly agreed, already feeling smitten by this headfast talented girl. After giving him her address, she told him her name. "I'm Frida Kahlo, by the way."

This name took a moment to resonate. Then he remembered his conversation with the school director many years ago. "Wait, but you're..."

Frida pressed her finger to his lips. "Yeah, so what? I was the girl in the auditorium. That has nothing to do with now. Do you still want to come Sunday or not?"

Diego had to hide the excitement in his voice for fear that his invitation might be rescinded. He simply answered, "Yes."

With that, Frida grabbed her canvases, refusing help from Rivera, and left. The large colored sails flapped in the wind from underneath her arms.

Diego arrived promptly that Sunday at the address given to him. His palms were beginning to sweat as he made his first knock on the door. Nervousness was building in his chest as he waited on this tantalizing girl to come to the threshold.

To his surprise, the answer came from above in a tree. He looked up to see the young woman dressed in overalls climbing down the branches. Frida landed and immediately opened the door. Giggling, she grabbed Diego by the hand and pulled him inside, quickly passing through the house to her bedroom.

As soon as they entered, she began parading painting after painting past the amused muralist. Her energy and excitement entranced the man twenty years her senior. By the time he could glance at a portrait, another was thrust into his lap. Diego met every person who was ever viewed through Frida's brush, including dozens of versions of herself. Her passion for art delighted the atmosphere. Once again, he was falling in love.

Diego returned daily in romantic pursuit of this enchanting young woman. Each visit, she would introduce him to another group of portraits, and he would offer complimented criticism. He mentored with a gentle hand of affection. This steadfast young woman was intoxicating, and time apart was sure to lead to withdrawals.

Frida continued to invite this man who viewed her work with honesty. There was a kindness to his criticism that evoked trust in his opinion. The two would spend hours discussing a single piece of work. Suggestion mixed with praise as the art took center stage of discourse.

On his fourth visit, they sat on the floor in front of Frida's most recent work. Side by side, they critiqued each layer. Diego pointed across his body to the upper right quadrant of the canvas. His shoulder rubbed Frida's and drew her eyes to his. The magnetic poles no longer had the distance to repel the attraction. The current slowly pulled the two closer. The distance diminished with barely a breath separating their lips from grazing. Then the magnetic field shattered, and their mouths embraced. The muralist pulled the young Frida closer as the world changed direction.

Within the year, Diego had left Guadalupe and their two children and married Frida, much to the disdain of their parents. Their tumultuous love affair would last until the death of Frida Kahlo. But even though their marriage was full of infidelity, by both parties, the two remained fervent that the other was the one that they were supposed to be with till the end.

David Zelnar

Thank you for joining me on this journey through Mexican history to witness a few of its tales that give a glimpse into the wonder of this fascinating country. I have done my best to keep these stories as close to the original folklore or history as possible. Tales give a glimpse into the perspective of those telling them. You can gain a further understanding of someone just by listening to his or her stories. Whether it be the lore of a group or the self-reflection of a person's day, having the intent to pay attention and comprehend the message the storyteller is attempting to portray will close the gap between us. It is this understanding that tears down walls. In my time in México, any preconceived notions I had soon melted away. It was by learning about the history and listening to story after story that I began to empathize at another level. Lending an ear is always reciprocated with access to a mismatched shoe.

David Zelnar

ABOUT THE AUTHOR

David Zelnar is from the United States. He studied history at the University of Florida. He has been abroad traveling and writing and teaching since 2014 looking for stories that capture his imagination. These stories come from while he was living in Guadalajara, Mexico.

Other Works

Adventures In Teaching:
> A Guide To Becoming An English Teacher Abroad

Land of the White Eagle:
> Legends of Polska

Śladami prozy Zbigniewa Białasa: (Korekta w języku angielskim)

Made in the USA
Monee, IL
26 October 2021